DINOSAUR DAYS
BRACHIOSAURUS

HEIGHT: 30′ (9.1 M)

HEIGHT: 5′ (1.5 M)

DINOSAUR DAYS
BRACHIOSAURUS

SARA GILBERT

CREATIVE EDUCATION CREATIVE PAPERBACKS

Table of Contents

Published by Creative Education
and Creative Paperbacks
P.O. Box 227, Mankato,
Minnesota 56002
Creative Education and Creative
Paperbacks are imprints of
The Creative Company
www.thecreativecompany.us

Book design by Blue Design
(www.bluedes.com)
Art direction by Rita Marshall
Printed in the United States of America

Photographs by Dreamstime
(Radiokafka), Thinkstock (Barks_japan,
chronicler101, CoreyFord, danku,
dottedhippo, Elenarts, Homunkulus28,
kotomiti, lenny777, leonello, lukaves,
MR1805, Pimpay, Vac1, Warpaintcobra),
Utah State Historical Society (Digital
Image © 2014 Utah State Historical
Society/Utah State Historical Society
Classified Photo Collection)

Library of Congress Cataloging-
in-Publication Data
Names: Gilbert, Sara, author.
Title: Brachiosaurus / Sara Gilbert.
Series: Dinosaur days.
Includes bibliographical
references and index.
Summary: This introductory
exploration uncovers the discovery
of *Brachiosaurus* fossils before
revealing information about its
era, features, and lifestyle, as
well as its eventual extinction.
Identifiers: ISBN 978-1-64026-
046-7 (hardcover) / ISBN 978-
1-62832-634-5 (pbk) / ISBN
978-1-64000-162-6 (eBook)

This title has been submitted for CIP
processing under LCCN 2018938948.

CCSS: RI.1.1, 2, 4, 5, 6, 7; RI.2.1, 2, 5, 6,
7; RI.3.1, 2, 5, 7; RF.1.1, 3, 4; RF.2.3, 4

First Edition HC 9 8 7 6 5 4 3 2 1
First Edition PBK 9 8 7 6 5 4 3 2 1

Meet *Brachiosaurus*!

Welcome to Museum für Naturkunde! We are the natural history museum in Berlin, Germany. You cannot miss our *Brachiosaurus* **skeleton**. It is the tallest dinosaur on display in the world!

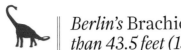

Berlin's Brachiosaurus *towers more than 43.5 feet (13.3 m) tall.*

Bigger than Big

Harold W. Menke found *Brachiosaurus* **fossils** in Colorado on July 4, 1900. The bones were huge! Some people thought it was the largest dinosaur ever. Its name means "arm lizard."

THE NECK OF A *BRACHIOSAURUS* COULD
BE 30 FEET (9.1 M) LONG.

Home on the Range

Brachiosaurus lived during the late Jurassic period. Its fossils have been found in western North America. Other giant **sauropods**, like *Supersaurus*, lived then, too.

SOUND-IT-OUT:

sauropods:
SAWR-uh-podz

HUNDREDS OF DINOSAUR FOSSILS WERE DISCOVERED IN THE LATE 1800S AND EARLY 1900S.

HUNDREDS OF DINOSAUR FOSSILS WERE DISCOVERED IN THE LATE 1800S AND EARLY 1900S.

SOUND-IT-OUT:

Jurassic:
jeh-RAS-ick

BRACHIOSAURUS — Home on the Range

BRACHIOSAURUS SWALLOWED FOOD WHOLE RATHER THAN CHEWING IT.

Reach for the Sky

Brachiosaurus could be 50 feet (15.2 m) tall. Its long neck could reach the tops of trees. Its front legs were longer than its back legs, like a giraffe!

Giant *Brachiosaurus* had a tiny head. A ridge stuck out from its forehead. Spoon-shaped teeth helped it tear leaves from trees.

227 MILLION YEARS AGO
LATE TRIASSIC

205 MILLION YEARS AGO
EARLY JURASSIC

180 MILLION YEARS AGO
MID-JURASSIC

Timeline

BRACHIOSAURUS LIVED HERE!

159 MILLION YEARS AGO
LATE JURASSIC

144 MILLION YEARS AGO
EARLY CRETACEOUS

98 MILLION YEARS AGO
LATE CRETACEOUS

In the Trees

Brachiosaurus ate plants. Some scientists say it could eat 500 pounds (227 kg) of food every day! A **herd** of *Brachiosaurus* would eat all the plants in an area.

A full-grown *Brachiosaurus* probably did not have any enemies. It was too big to be hunted by other dinosaurs.

Its long neck allowed the dinosaur to reach food high in trees and on the ground.

BECAUSE OF ITS BULKY BODY,
BRACHIOSAURUS LIKELY PREFERRED
FLAT LAND.

Bye, *Brachiosaurus*

At the end of the Jurassic, *Brachiosaurus* died out. Most of the other sauropods did, too. No one is sure what happened. Someday, maybe new clues will tell us why *Brachiosaurus* is **extinct**.

Glossary

extinct — a family or group having no more living members

fossils — bones or plants preserved for millions of years

herd — a group of animals that live together

sauropods — plant-eating dinosaurs that had long necks and tails, small heads, and five-toed feet

skeleton — the bones that support a body

Read More

Holtz, Thomas R., Jr. *Digging for Brachiosaurus: A Discovery Timeline*. North Mankato, Minn.: Capstone Press, 2015.

West, David. *Dinosaurs of the Jurassic*. Mankato, Minn.: Smart Apple Media, 2015.

Websites

DK Find Out!: Brachiosaurus
https://www.dkfindout.com/us/dinosaurs-and-prehistoric-life/dinosaurs/brachiosaurus/
Look at a diagram of *Brachiosaurus*, and take a dinosaur quiz.

National Geographic Kids: Brachiosaurus
https://kids.nationalgeographic.com/animals/brachiosaurus/#brachiosasurs.jpg
Learn more about *Brachiosaurus* and other dinosaurs.